HOW TO SKI THE BUMPS

By Bill Gulino

Sun Valley Publishing, Seattle, WA

Acknowledgements

Cover Design, Typography.
Typographics, Ketchum, Idaho
Printed by: Pro-Litho, Inc., Seattle

Cover Photo: By Janet Mahr. Author is negotiating modern style bump configurations on Lower Holiday in Sun Valley, Idaho.

Photographed Skiers:
    Kevin Embree   Carl Praeger
    David Gulino   Rick Swegel
    Jim Freeman   John Zuck
    Mike McCarthy

Special thanks to the following Sun Valley skiers for their contributions:
    Barbara Cordeau   Carl Praeger
    Kevin Embree   Curt Tempel
    Mike McCarthy   John Zuck

SUN VALLEY PUBLISHING
Seattle, Washington

Copyright © 1984 by Bill Gulino. All rights reserved. No portion of this book may be reproduced in any form or by any means without written permission of the publisher, except by a reviewer, who may quote brief passages in a review. First edition. First printing, November 1984. Second printing, October 1985. Third printing, August 1987.

ISBN 0-915803-01-1

Contents

Foreward: About this book and its author v
Chapter 1. Skis and Equipment 7
Chapter 2. Beginning Bump Skiing Technique—
            Skiing the Ruts 9
Chapter 3. Modern Bump Configurations 13
Chapter 4. The Theory Behind Modern Bump Skiing 17
Chapter 5. How to Ski out of the Ruts—
            The Essence of Modern Bump Skiing 19
Chapter 6. How to Make Controlled Turns
            in the Bumps 23
Chapter 7. How to Absorb and Extend in Big Bumps 31
Chapter 8. The Importance of the Pole Plant 37
Chapter 9. How to Ski Different
            Snow Conditions in the Bumps 41
Chapter 10. How to Get Air in the Bumps 43
Chapter 11. A Few Pointers on
            Skiing the Bumps Safely 49
Chapter 12. How to Get in Shape
            for Skiing the Bumps 51
Chapter 13. Ten Common Errors Made
            When Skiing in the Bumps 55
Chapter 14. Conclusion - Self Evaluation 59

Foreward: About This Book and Its Author

Bumps! To many recreational skiers, and to many professional skiers as well, this word represents the ultimate skiing challenge. Because bump skiing is an advanced aspect of the sport, the text in this book is intended for those skiers who have mastered the basic techniques of parallel skiing. This is not a book on learning how to ski! But rather, it is a guide for the experienced skier—the skier who wants to know how to improve on his or hers already acquired skills to ski the bumps proficiently. The techniques described in this book are those currently used by professional mogul skiing champions.

The information in this book is based on what could be called a "sub-culture" of skiers that live in Sun Valley, Idaho. This group of skiers spend their winters skiing the bumps on Baldy. With the development of modern style bumps and the hard-pack snow conditions that can occur on Baldy, new bump skiing techniques were necessary. Over the last ten years this "sub-culture" of bump skiers in Sun Valley have developed the new techniques to ski the bumps smoothly and proficiently. These new techniques have taken mogul skiing past the confinements of standard ski school teachings.

During this time I have watched these new bump skiing trends emerge. I have also skied in professional bump competitions as well. I feel fortunate to have observed, given input, and generally been a part of this bump skiing "sub-culture" in Sun Valley, Idaho.

Unlike most ski books which have the tendency of being too wordy, this book will offer specific pointers. In this way the reader's mind will not be cluttered with over analyzations. Specific pointers are presented in clear language so the reader can understand what is being said. An thus, the reader can easily incorporate the information into his or hers skiing technique.

Bill Gulino

Chapter #1

Skis and Equipment

If a skier is having a hard time skiing the bumps, often frustration will lead him to blame his equipment for his difficulties.* One will hear excuses like, "My skis are too long for these bumps," or "My boots are too loose." This leads one to believe that it could never be the skier. Right? However, in all fairness, sometimes skis or equipment are to blame for a skier's frustration to skiing the bumps. To ski the bumps confidently requires the proper equipment. Improper or inadequate equipment can hamper a skier's ability to ski the bumps well. Here are some suggestions on what competitive bump skiers consider to be important criteria when it comes to bump skiing equipment.

SKIS: The era of the short ski has passed for bump skiing. A good bump ski length for most men is between 200 cm. and 204 cm. A good bump ski length for most women is around 190 cm. Also, a bump ski should be fiberglass and not metal. Competitive bump skiers believe fiberglass at the above mentioned lengths make a ski turn quickly while still providing stability. Another important point why a ski should be fiberglass and not metal is a metal ski stands a good chance of bending or delaminating if skied hard in the bumps. A metal ski just doesn't have the durability or quickness that a fiberglass ski has when it comes to bump skiing.

Some competitive bump skiers prefer giant slalom (G.S.) skis, while other competitive bump skiers prefer slalom skis. The bump skiers who ski on G.S. skis do so because they like the even flex that is characteristic of G.S. skis. The bump skiers who ski on slalom skis like the quick turning capabilities of slalom skis. It's just a matter of personal preference.

---

*For the sake of convenience, and in order to avoid having to say his or hers all the time, I am going to resort to the accepted grammatical standard and use the masculine pronoun. This does not mean bump skiing is for men only. There are plenty of women who are excellent skiers. These women could probably teach some of the guys a few things about skiing bumps. Using the masculine gender is for ease of writing only.

POLES: There are three important elements that a ski pole should have for skiing bumps. First, a ski pole should be a high quality aluminum so that it is light weight. Second, a ski pole should have a platform strap grip. And third, a ski pole should have a small stiff plastic basket.

The light weight obviously allows a skier to swing the pole more quickly, but more important than light weight is the grip and the basket.

The grip should be a platform strap grip. This enables the skier the get good swing and reach in his pole plant. A grip should not be the "strapless" or "saber" type grip. This type of grip hinders a good swing and reach in a pole plant, and encourages a skier to ski with the palms of his hands facing forward. This is called "open-palmed." I will talk about skiing "open-palmed" in more detail in the chapter on pole planting. But, skiing "open-palmed" lends itself to letting the hands get back. And once the hands get back skiing bumps, the skier is back on his skis.

The common concern among competitive bump skiers about a ski pole basket is whether or not it provides a good pole plant. Sometimes if a pole plant is made on the crest or back side of a bump, some pole baskets will skip the pole tip off the snow. This results in a missed pole plant. A missed pole plant in the bumps can throw a skier's rhythm off or even cause him to fall. I have personally taken full on "headers" in the bumps as a result of a missed pole plant caused by a "skipping" basket. The worst offender for skipping is the large plastic snowflake type basket. The smaller sized (about 3" dia.) stiff plastic basket does a much better job of setting the pole tip into the snow.

BOOTS AND BINDINGS: Ski boots and bindings should be good quality, especially since bump skiing puts a greater demand on durability of ski equipment than normal recreational skiing.

Boots should have a good comfortable fit, and not lose lateral support when flexed forward. Also, a ski boot should have a medium, but not too soft, forward flex. When it comes to priorities in a ski boot for skiing bumps one pro bump skier so appropriately stated, "the fit is number one!"

There is really nothing special about bindings for skiing bumps that is different from conventional recreational skiing. Bindings should be high performance, but designed for a skier's weight and ability.

Chapter #2

Beginning Bump Skiing Technique—Skiing the Ruts

When first learning how to ski bumps, most ski instructors will teach their pupils how to ski *around* the bumps. Skiing around the bumps is the basic philosophy of how to ski moguls. This results in the beginning bump skier skiing the troughs or "ruts." When first learning how to ski bumps this is a good technique because it works well in small bumps. The best place to first learn how to ski bumps is in small bumps anyway.

However, in big or modern style bumps that can be "chopped-off" or deeply rutted, the novice bump skier soon realizes skiing the "ruts" is not only difficult, but physically punishing as well. A skier who skis these types of bumps by only skiing in the "ruts" has the tendency to "pound" or "tail-slap" his way down the mountain. He can't help but drop down into one "rut" after another. Using hip projection will make skiing deep "ruts" a smoother ride however. But, to ski large or modern style bumps proficiently, the advanced bump skier has to be able to ski the sides and tops of the bumps as well. The techniques of hip projection and skiing out of the "ruts" will be discussed later.

But for now, most beginning bump skiers find it easier to first learn how to ski around the bumps before they can master the more advanced techniques of skiing the sides and tops of the bumps. Skiing around the bumps or in the "ruts" will later serve as only *part* of the advanced skier's total repertoire.

Fig. 2-1—The skier absorbs the bump with his lower body-that primarily being his legs, knees, and ankles. He also plants the pole on top of the bump so as to initiate a turn around the bump.

Fig. 2-2—The skier continues his turn by sliding down the side of the bump into the trough or "rut."

Fig. 2-3—After making a strong edge set against the bump (as shows in Fig. 2-1), the skier initiates his next turn in the other direction. He will continue his path of skiing by sliding down the side of the bump into the next "rut."

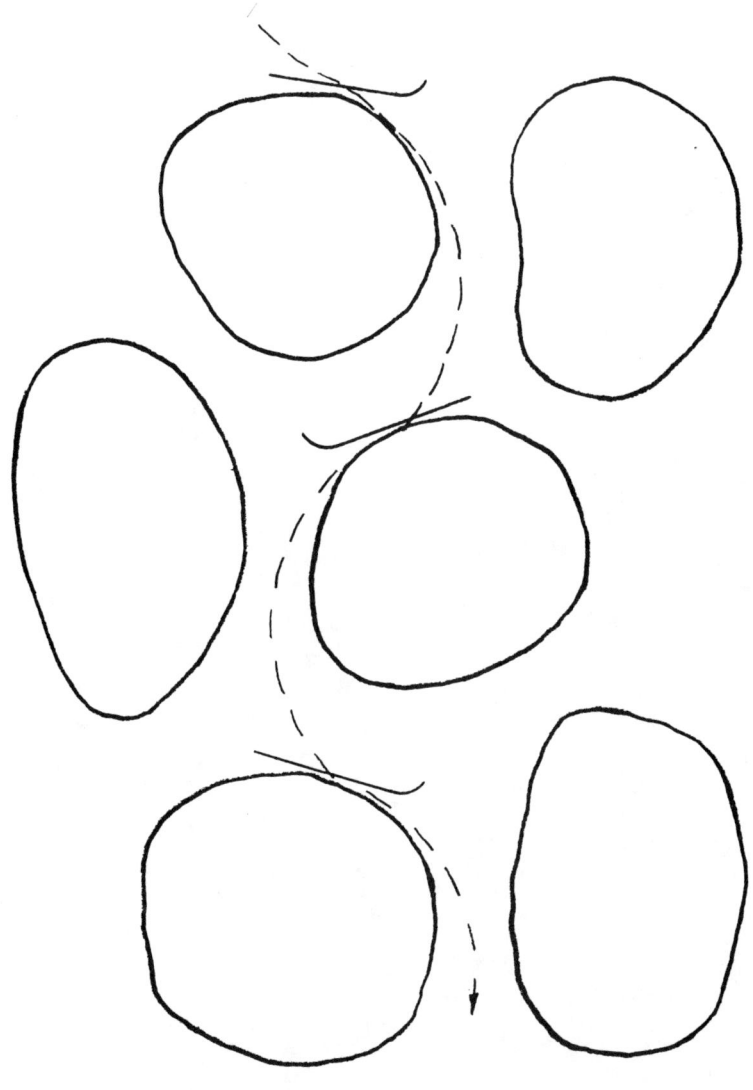

SKIING THE "RUTS"—The beginning bump skier often finds skiing **around** the bumps or in the "ruts" the easiest way to first learn how to ski moguls. This technique will later serve as only **part** of the advanced skier's total repertoire.

Chapter #3
Modern Bump Configurations

When looking at different types of bumps there seems to be little consistency to their shapes and patterns. They look more like abstract art than moguls. However, there are a couple of specific bump formations that are reoccurring and can be talked about independently. These formations have made skiing bumps more difficult. When skiing modern style bumps, the skier will inevitably encounter these conditions: "ruts," "holes," and "vertical side walls."

Irregular shapes and patternings are typical of modern bump configurations.

Examples of modern bump configurations in Sun Valley, Idaho.

Exhibition

Lower Holiday

Limelight

Lower Holiday

Upper River Run

Lower Holiday

RUTS: "Ruts" refer to the trough areas between the bumps. As the "ruts" become deeper and deeper, they become more punishing to ski. Skiing deep "ruts" is like skiing a staircase. The skier drops down from platform to platform unable to get much deflection from the skis. The reason for this is because the tails of the skis get caught in-between the bumps. As a result, the skier has a difficult time controlling his speed, and often just "tail-slaps" from one bump to the next. To correct this situation the skier needs to ski the sides and tops of the bumps. (See chapter 5, "How To Ski Out Of The Ruts—The Essence Of Modern Bump Skiing.")

HOLES: Sometimes a certain spot on a bump run will get more dug out than another, and literally a "hole" will develop. A "hole" is really just a term used by bump skiers to describe an extra deep trough. However, this exaggerated trough condition appears more like a "hole" because a large bump is on the other side of it, making the situation even more imposing to ski. When a skier encounters this situation he should not drop too far down into the trough or "hole." He can also avoid the situation by jumping over it. (See chapter 5, "How to Ski Out Of The Ruts—The Essence Of Modern Bump Skiing," and chapter 10, "How To Get Air In The Bumps.")

VERTICAL SIDE WALLS: Sometimes, if a particular bump has received alot of skier traffic it will develop steep or "vertical side walls." When a bump has "vertical side walls" it is often referred to as being "chopped-off." When a skier encounters a "vertical side wall" while skiing the bumps, a good way to handle the situation is with a banking type turn. (See chapter 5, "How To Ski Out Of The Ruts—The Essence Of Modern Bump Skiing.")

To ski modern bumps requires using a variety of techniques. These techniques are discussed in more detail in the chapters that follow.

Chapter #4
The Theory Behind Modern Bump Skiing

The theory behind modern bump skiing is learning how to ski *out of the "ruts."*

During the last several years many skiers have been baffled by the contorted and irregular shapes of the bumps. This has inevitably made them more difficult to ski. Some people blame these new bump configurations on "hacker" type skiers who are on short skis. Personally, I think it has more to do with increased skier traffic and improvements in ski equipment. These two factors have permitted more skiers to make more turns on the bump runs. For whatever reason, the bumps today are often irregular in shape, closer together, deeply rutted, big, "chopped-off," unrhythmical, and generally more complex to ski. As a result, the old standard bump skiing philosophy of skiing the "ruts" has only limited application.

The old standard bump skiing philosophy advocates that the skier should ski around the bumps. The skier is taught to absorb the bump, turn on the top, and slide down the side into the trough. (See chapter 2, "Beginning Bump Skiing Technique—Skiing The Ruts.") This results in having the skier ski in the "ruts." Under some situations this technique is applicable. Under some situations it is not! Skiing around the bumps or in the "ruts" serves well as a beginning bump skiing technique or when the bumps are small. However, when the bumps are bigger and more irregular in shape and pattern, this technique of skiing the "ruts" can't always be used effectively. To ski the bumps proficiently today, the bump skier must learn a variety of techniques to handle the irregularities of modern moguls. This means putting less emphasis on skiing the "ruts," and learning to ski the sides and the tops of the bumps.

Chapter #5

How To Ski Out Of The Ruts—
The Essence Of Modern Bump Skiing

To ski modern bumps proficiently, the skier has to be able to ski out of the "ruts." To do this, the skier needs to use techniques that will enable him to ski the sides and tops of the bumps.

To Ski The Sides Of The Bumps— Use Banking Type Turns

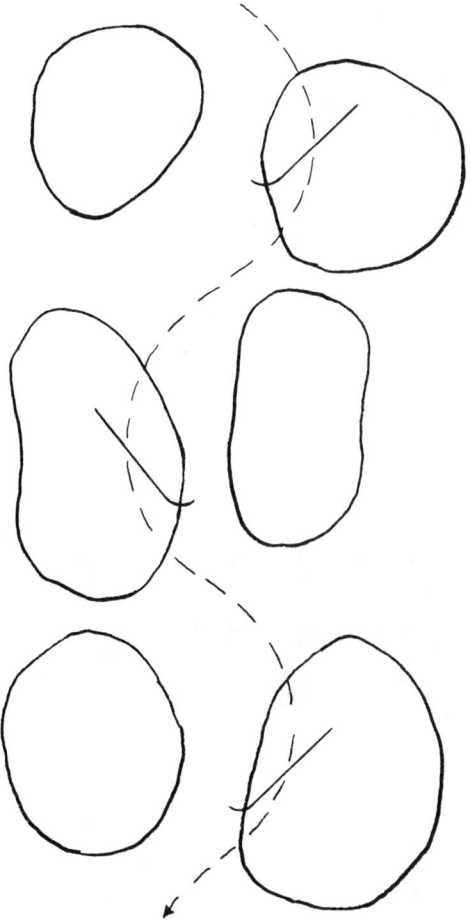

To get out of the "ruts" by skiing the sides of the bumps, the skier literally has to bank his turns off the sides of the bumps. The skier doesn't want to lean into the hill, however. He still needs to maintain his angulation. For those skiers who are familiar with racing, banking turns off the sides of the bumps is like banking turns off the sides of deep ruts on a heavily skied race course.

Also, a banking type turn comes in handy when a skier encounters a "chopped-off" bump with a vertical side wall. The skier can handle the situation by making a quick banking type turn off the side of it. Or, if a skier encounters a deep "hole" or "rut", he can use a banking type turn off an adjacent bump to swing wide of the "hole."

To Ski The Tops Of The Bumps— Cut Across The Ruts

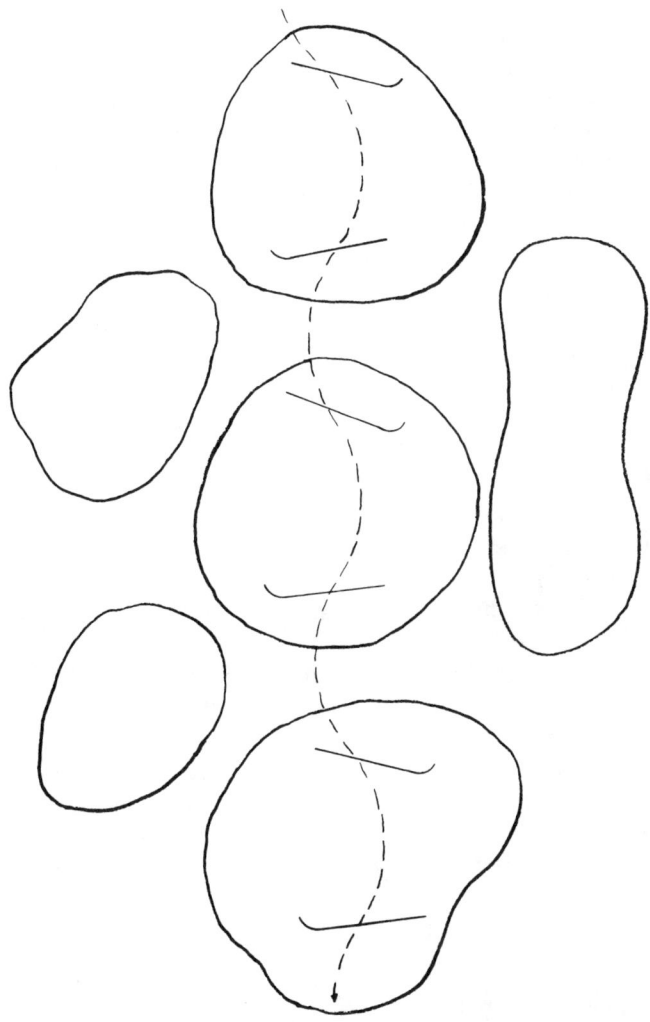

To ski the tops of the bumps, the skier has to perform a particular sequence. First, the skier cuts across the "rut" to take him up the front side and to the top of that bump. Then, he maintains his turning rhythm by making another turn on the back side of the same bump.

This results in the skier coming out of the "ruts" and enabling him to make two turns per bump. This technique works especially well in big bumps. Big bumps have a lot of room on the tops for making turns.

The Final Product— A Mixed Bag Of Tricks

In chapter two, I talked about how skiing the "ruts" serves well as a beginning bump skiing technique. In this chapter, however, I emphasize to ski modern bumps proficiently, the more advanced bump skier has to be able to ski *out of the "ruts."* More specifically, he has to be able to ski the sides and tops of the bumps also.

However, I have yet to mention how to apply these techniques in a sequence or pattern. In other words, how to pick a line in the bumps. I haven't offered this advise for a good reason. There is just no way to constantly predict where the next turn is going to be made when skiing bumps aggressively. The next turn may need to be made in a "rut", on the top of a bump, or off the side of a bump. To do this a skier needs to be able to ski everywhere on a bump.

Most top bump skiers may plan their first one or two turns, but after that their runs are spontaneous. Because of the irregular shapes and patterns of modern style bumps, a skier needs to be spontaneous. With a variety of techniques, he can deal spontaneously to *situations.* He doesn't have to rely on a "good line" to make his turns for him.

If a skier knows how to ski the "ruts", ski the sides of the bumps, and ski the tops of the bumps, this will greatly increase his opportunities for making a turn. Then he will be able to spontaneously react to different situations as he encounters them. This will increase his control and ability of skiing modern style bumps. Being spontaneous with a variety of techniques to handle the irregularities of today's bumps is the essence of modern bump skiing.

Fig. 5-1—Cutting across the "rut."

Fig. 5-2—Making a turn on the back side of a bump. A good example of hip projection. (See chapter 7, "How to Absorb and Extend in Big Bumps")

Fig. 5-3—Banking a turn off the side of a bump. Note the skier still maintains angulation.

Fig. 5-4—Sliding down the side of a bump into the "rut."

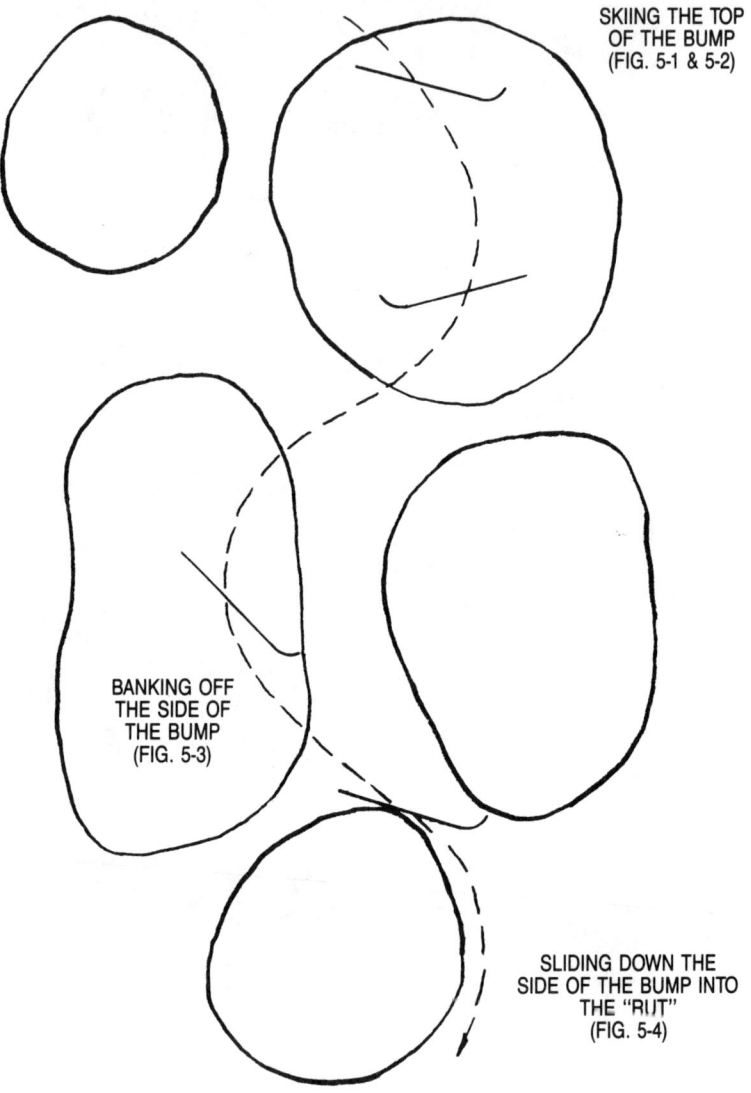

Fig. 5-5—Because of the irregular shapes and patterns of modern style bumps, a skier needs to be spontaneous. With a variety of techniques, he can deal spontaneously to **situations**.

Chapter #6

How To Make Controlled Turns In The Bumps

When people ask me to give them tips on skiing bumps, they often want to know what is the secret. The first thing I tell them is that the same basic skiing techniques they use on groomed runs can be applied to the bumps. Their response usually is that they can ski groomed runs fine, but once they get into the bumps everything falls apart. Therefore, there must be something different required for bump skiing than there is for other aspects of recreational skiing. There is no question that there are some specific techniques required for skiing bumps. However, one very predominate factor about skiing bumps that is different from skiing groomed runs is a skier's margin of error is greatly decreased.

For example, if a skier doesn't edge strongly enough on groomed runs, there is generally a lot of room to slow down, come across the hill, and time to regain control. The skier's error is of little concern and probably will go unnoticed. On a bump run, however, the same mistake would be magnified and could result in the skier losing total control. In other words, on groomed runs a skier's weaknesses in his skiing technique can literally go unnoticed. However, once in the bumps, these weaknesses become very evident. Even proficient bump skiers that are having a hard day or who seem to have reached a plateau in their skiing are often overlooking a basic skiing skill.

A skier must first refine the basic skiing techniques on terrain he feels comfortable with before he can expect to ski bumps well. A skier must first practice and be able to make short swing turns on groomed runs. After that, he can then attempt to make the same carved or edge-setting type turns with consistant rhythm in the bumps.

The advanced bump skier today makes great use of his skis just as a slalom racer would. Although a ski turn is different in the bumps than it is on a race course, both skiers make their skis work for them so they can get as much efficiency as possible from every turn.

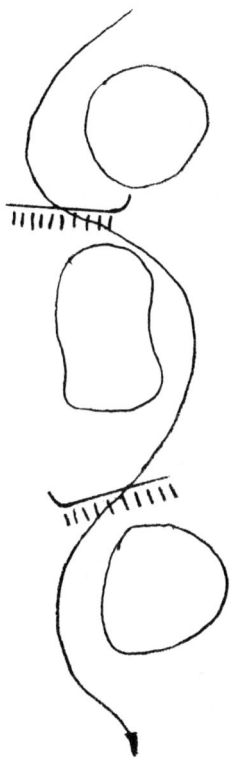

*The glide vs. the check. The biggest difference between a good racing turn and a good bump skiing turn is where the energy is placed in the turn. In a racing turn, the energy is placed in the beginning to middle of the turn. The ski racer wants to hold an edge and then **glide out** of the turn. Whereas the bump skier wants to create a **checking** action with his skis. The bump skier puts energy at the end of the turn.*

The biggest difference between a good racing turn and a good bump skiing turn is where the energy is placed in the turn. In a racing turn, the energy is placed in the beginning to the middle of the turn. The ski racer wants to hold an edge and then *glide* out of the turn. Whereas the bump skier wants to create a *checking* action with his skis. The bump skier puts energy at the end of the turn.

The reasons for these differences is because a ski racer is trying to increase speed through the gates by accelerating out of his turns. The bump skier, however, is in constant battle with gravity to maintain a controlled speed over a much more irregular terrain. From what I have observed, this explains why many bump skiers have slow times when they ski gates, and why many racers find skiing bumps difficult. Bump skiers slow themselves down too much with checking type turns on a race course. And racers, when they get into the bumps, tend to skip from bump to bump because they are gliding or accelerating out of their turns. Instead, ski racers should use a checking action at the end of the turn to maintain a controlled or constant speed in the bumps.

The point of this discussion is to make it clear that a bump skier needs to know how to use his skis effectively to get the best results skiing the bumps. A bump skier wants to get energy and deflection from his skis. By the term deflection, I mean having the skis carve or make an edge-setting type turn across the fall line. The bumps skier does not want to just "tail-slap" his way down a bump run. By "tail-slap," I mean pounding down the bumps with the skis not getting much deflection, if not literally just pointed straight down the hill. Some bump skiers seem to get away with the "tail-slapping" technique if the snow is soft. However, when the snow conditions are firm, "tail-slapping" proves to be ineffective as well as "self-abusive."

Learning how to make the skis work for the skier gives him an advantage when dealing with a variety of snow conditions and the irregularities of today's bumps.

Chapter #7

How To Absorb And Extend In Big Bumps

A skier's body has to have the ability to absorb and extend over the irregularities in terrain. A skier's body being able to act like a "shock absorber" is a fundamental principle of skiing. Any skier who has taken a ski lesson was introduced to this fundamental principle when his instructor told him to bend his knees. However, there is a big difference between absorbing and extending in conventional skiing, and absorbing and extending in big bumps. In big bumps a skier has to be able to absorb and extend ALOT MORE.

Most skiers absorb a bump well, but they often just don't get enough extension. An error I often see with beginning to intermediate bump skiing enthusiasts is they don't properly extend on the back side of a bump. A skier who does not get good extension on the back side of a bump usually has the following skiing problems. First, he has the tendency to get knocked back on his skis. By not extending properly, a skier fails to stay forward on his skis. Secondly, if a skier does not get good extension on the back side of a bump he also has a difficult time controlling his speed in the bumps. If a skier does not get good extension, his skis will lose contact with the snow when he should be completing his turns.

To get the needed extension on the back side of a bump a skier needs to drop his ski tips down and get good *hip projection*. Hip projection is when the skier pushes the hips forward after coming over the top of a bump. This action keeps the skier forward on his skis. The hips are pushed forward, the legs are extended, and the tips of the skis are dropped down to maintain contact with the snow. Hip projection is essential to skiing big bumps successfully.

I believe the reason most skiers don't get good extension in the bumps is because of apprehension. The idea of falling over one's ski tips acts as a mental block in keeping many skiers from pushing their hips forward and dropping their tips down on the back side of a bump. When a skier is in an unsure situation, like big bumps, the natural reaction is to sit back on the heels, and get the skis out front. The last thing a skier's subconscious wants him to do is to push the hips forward, extend the legs, and press on the balls of the feet to drop the tips of the skis down to the snow. But this is what a skier is precisely to do. In the radical terrain of big bumps, this is the only way to get enough extension to act as an effective "shock absorber."

To get confident at hip projection, practice the technique in small bumps. The motion required in small bumps will not be as exaggerated as it is in larger bumps. But a skier can build his confidence there before working his way up to more demanding terrain.

There is one final point about absorbing and extending in the bumps I would like to make. The motion is done with the lower body: the hips, legs, knees, and ankles. This may be an obvious statement, but many skiers will mistakenly absorb a bump by bending forward at the waist. Trying to absorb a bump by bending forward at the waist will often put a skier off balance. Bending forward at the waist to absorb a bump makes it difficult for the skier to get full extension in the moment that follows. Keep a quiet upper body, and let the legs do all the ups and downs.

Absorption

ABSORPTION—When absorbing a big bump keep a quite upper body. The motion of absorbing and extending over a bump is done with the lower body—the hips, legs, knees, and ankles.

Extension

EXTENSION—To ski big bumps well, a skier has to drive the tips of his skis down the back sides of the bumps. This is accomplished by getting good hip projection.

HIP PROJECTION is when the skier pushes the hips forward after coming over the top of a bump. This action keeps the skier forward on his skis. The hips are pushed forward, the legs are extended, and the tips of the skis are dropped down the back side of the bump so they maintain contact with the snow.

Chapter #8
The Importance Of The Pole Plant

Keeping the hands forward is imperative to skiing the bumps aggressively! If a skier finds himself getting back on his skis it may be he is not driving forward with his hands. The secret to driving forward with the hands is centered in the pole plant.

If a skier's hands are getting back in the bumps, the cause many times is he does not reach out far enough with the pole plant. If a skier does not get enough reach with the pole plant in the bumps, he will ski past his pole plant before he has completed it. This will inevitably draw the hand back to the side, if not even farther behind. Remember, even if a hand gets to the side of the body when skiing bumps, this will put the skier back on his skis.

To get a good pole plant in the bumps, the skier has to reach out with the pole tip. A skier should concentrate on making the pole plant out about the distance of his ski tip. A skier should not plant the pole straight down by the boot. Literally, the skier should swing the pole out nearly its full length. However, the skier does not want to bend over at the waist to get the reach with the pole plant. This will put him off balance. The reach does not come from the shoulder, but rather it comes with the flick of the wrist. This is the reason for the platform strap grip. A pole with a platform strap grip enables the skier to get the needed flick of the wrist and swinging action in the pole plant.

Another point about the pole plant is the skier should be "closed palmed." "Closed palmed" is where the elbows are out and the hands are in, what you could call, a boxer's position. The knuckles of the hands are facing out to the sides. The converse, "open palmed," is where the skier pushes the palms of his hands facing forward. When a skier is skiing "open palmed" the knuckles of the hands are pointed backward. An "open palmed" position inevitably brings the elbows in close to the body and encourages the skier to drop the hands back.

Why would a skier use an "open palmed" position? Subconsciously, it is done to get the needed reach in the pole plant. "Open palmed" skiers are usually a product of the "saber" or "strapless" type grip. These grips do not facilitate a flick of the wrist and swinging action needed in a bump skiing pole plant. As a result, the bump skier inadvertently tries to get the reach by bending the wrists back and facing the palms forward. This does get the desired reach, unfortunately, it also encourages the skier to drop the hands back. To remedy this, use a platform strap grip that gives a good swinging action.

Finally, always think about driving forward with the hands, and the pole plants are usually made on the tops of the bumps.

Fig. 8-1—Reach out with the pole plant! Getting a good reach in the pole plant helps keep the hands forward. Remember, even if a hand gets to the side of the body when skiing bumps, this will put the skier back on his skis.

Fig. 8-2, -3—Examples of bump skiers reaching out with their pole plants.

Fig. 8-4—"Open palmed" is where the skier pushes the palms of his hands facing forward. An "open palmed" position inevitably brings the elbows in close to the body and encourages the skier to drop the hands back. Once the hands are back skiing bumps, the skier is back on his skis.

Fig. 8-5—"Closed palmed" is where the elbows are out and the hands are in, what could be called, a boxer's position. The "closed palmed" position encourages the skier to drive forward with his hands.

Chapter #9

How To Ski Different Snow Conditions In The Bumps

POWDER BUMPS: My favorite conditions to ski are soft powder bumps. They are forgiving and exciting to ski. However, there are a few pointers to keep in mind if the skier wants to get the most enjoyment out of skiing these types of bumps well.

In soft powder bumps, a hard edge set is not as important as it is on harder snow. As a matter of fact, the skier wants to avoid over-turning his skis. The skier doesn't need to get much deflection from his skis when skiing powder bumps. He can let the skis run. The skier can control his speed by running straight into the fronts of the bumps. The skier should keep his skis in the fall line, and ski from top to top. One pro bump skier described skiing powder bumps by saying, "I just leave my feet more under my hips and ride the waves."

The skier should stay centered over the skis. This is accomplished by maintaining even pressure on the balls and heels of the feet. Although, sometimes I will put a little more pressure on the balls of my feet, if I want to drop the tips of my skis down the back side of a bump. But, the skier should be cautious not to get too far forward or he may take a "header" if he suddenly hits deeper snow.

Finally, be fairly even-weighted on the skis. At least more so than on harder snow. However, the skier should be careful not to let the uphill ski transfer his weight into the hill. This will cause the skier to lean into the hill and problems such as crossing tails and getting knocked-back on the skis can occur. Putting too much weight on the uphill ski can even cause the skis to come out from underneath the skier on a steep bump.

ICY BUMPS: Skiing icy or hard snow bumps can be intimidating. The first trick to skiing these types of bumps proficiently is to have WELL-TUNED SKIS! It can be a chore sometimes, and I'm probably one of the worst offenders to ski maintenance. But, I can say from experience, sharp edges make a big difference. On hard snow, the skier needs to get a good bite with his skis. If his edges are dull, the skis will slip or slide in the turns. This makes it difficult for the skier to get enough of an edge set to control speed.

A second important point to skiing icy bumps is to ski them at slower speeds. Control is the name of the game here. A skier just can't safely let his skis run and hope to control his speed by running into a bump as he would in softer snow conditions.

When making turns in icy bumps, the skier should be more forward than he would be in powder or slush bumps. Also, the skier should get more deflection from his skis by carving the turns more across the fall line than in softer snow conditions. Skiing hard snow conditions also requires more independent leg action. This means more weight on the downhill ski and less emphasis on even-weighting as in powder bump conditions.

SLUSH BUMPS: Many of the same principles for skiing powder bumps also apply to skiing slush bumps. There is one big difference, however. When skiing slush bumps, the skier decelerates faster in the turns than on powder bumps. This means the skier's turns have to be rounder and not have radical edge sets. Because slush snow is grabby the skier has to be "soft-footed."

As with powder bumps, the skier should keep a center-of-balance. And, he should be more even-weighted on his skis than on icy or hard snow bumps. But, he should still be conscious of maintaining independent leg action by keeping a little more weight on the downhill ski.

The skier can run straight into slush bumps to control speed as with powder bumps. However, more caution is advised if the back sides of the bumps are shaded from the warm spring-time sun. These areas could be icy.

Chapter #10

How To Get Air In The Bumps

Getting air in the bumps is not only exciting, but it is also functional. A bump skier who knows how to jump in the bumps can avoid situations like deep "holes" and "ruts" by jumping over them. Also, the skier can spontaneously change his line by jumping laterally.

Here are the basic points of how to get air in the bumps:

1. First, spot the bump where you want to get air.
2. Second, spot the landing. This is done almost simultaneously with spotting the bump where you want to get air.

The real secret to getting good air in the bumps is developing the ability to spot and make a precision landing. When landing a jump in a close knit set of bumps there isn't much margin for error. Being off just a little bit can put a skier into a deep "hole" or "rut." A bump skier should always know where he will land *before* he gets air off a bump. To develop this intuition takes practice and experience.

3. Jump at the top of the bump. This will give the skier more spring or "pop" in his jump. Also, the skier wants to jump "up" and not so much "out." Bumps with steep fronts will facilitate this upward motion. However, the first priority of a skier's angle of projectile is to reach the predetermined landing bump.

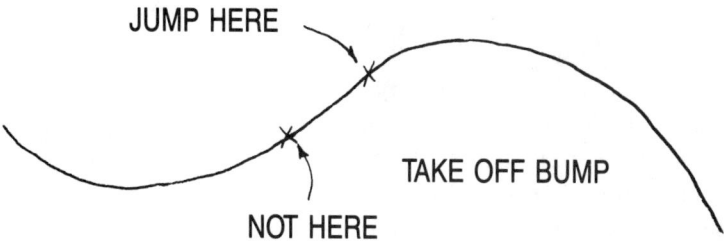

4. The spring obviously comes from the legs. Keep the hands in front! Note: in some tip-dropping type air tricks, the bump skiing aerialist will either raise one or both hands (depending on the maneuver) over his head. This counteracts the tip-dropping motion of the trick so as to maintain aerial balance. However, the airborne bump skier should always land with both feet on the snow and with at least one pole plant.

5. Land on top of the bump. A skier should try to avoid landing in a "hole" or "rut." This will make the landing considerably more difficult. When the bumps are soft, as with powder or slush snow, the skier should try to land his jump more on the top-front side of the bump. And when the snow is firm, the skier should try to land more on the top-back side of the bump.

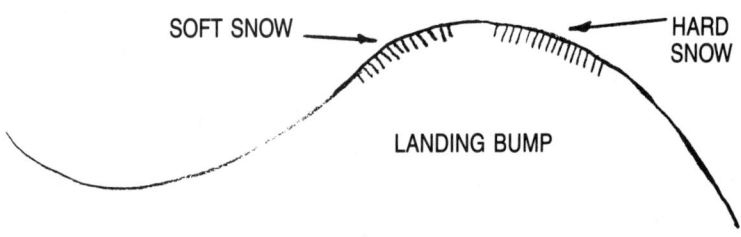

6. Land in a turn. This is very important, especially in harder snow conditions. This is done by landing with the skis starting across the fall line and on edge. Weight should be primarily on the downhill ski in the landing. However, in softer snow conditions such as powder or slush, the skier can land with the skis pointed more down the fall line. The cushion of the soft snow will help control the skier's speed.

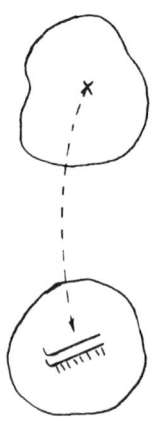

Land in a turn!

7. Jumping laterally. When jumping in the bumps, the skier sometimes finds it necessary to jump to the side. I call this lateral air projection. This type of air is still primarily down the fall line, however, the skier's destination is one or two bumps over to the side. Lateral air projection facilitates landing on the edge of the skis, and is useful when a skier wants to change his line. Generally, a bump skier can jump straight down the fall line when the snow conditions are soft. However, when the snow conditions are firm, lateral air projection facilitates landing on the edge of the skis and makes landing in hard bumps less brutal.

Getting air in the bumps is an advanced bump skiing skill! Therefore, a skier should have an accurate perception of his skiing ability before he starts thinking about jumping in the bumps. It seems that some people have a better "air sense" than others. If a skier feels uneasy in the air, it is best that skier stay on the snow.

To develop "air sense," a skier should first practice jumps when the bumps are soft powder snow conditions. If it seems to the skier that he can develop an "air sense," then he can go ahead and practice getting air in other types of snow conditions.

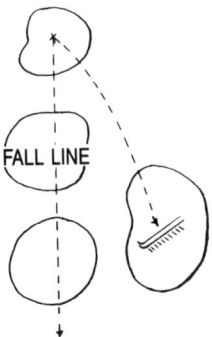

45

Tip-crosser

Twister

Spread Eagle

THE SPREAD EAGLE - The spread eagle is a classic bump skiing aerial maneuver. It seems every bump skier has his own individual version of how the trick should be performed.

Chapter #11

A Few Pointers
On Skiing The Bumps Safely

Skiing the bumps, just like any other athletic activity, can become dangerous if the proper safety precautions are not taken. The smart bump skier incorporates the following practices into his mogul skiing itinerary:

1. Be in good physical condition. Any skier that doesn't spend some time in the preseason getting in shape for skiing, let alone skiing the bumps, is asking for trouble. A well-conditioned body is less susceptible to injury. That is a fact! Note: It should be stated here that bump skiing is a physically demanding sport. If the skier has any health problems, he should first consult a physician before skiing bumps.

2. Know your skiing ability. Although bump skiing is a "go for it" type sport, the wreckless bump skier will increase his chance of injury. The bump skier who skis within his ability will reduce the chance of an injury while still building a foundation of skiing technique. A good foundation of skiing technique enables the skier to explore new limits in his skiing abilities safely.

3. Be conscious of skier traffic. Sometimes skiers on a bump run get in each other's way. To avoid collisions, always practice the following:

    A. DO - Look up the hill before you start to ski.
    B. DO - Ski slowly when approaching other skiers, intersections, or congested areas.
    C. DON'T - Stand in areas where descending skiers can't see you.
    D. DON'T - Traverse into another skier's line of skiing.
    E. DON'T - Jump blindly.

Consideration for your fellow bump skier will make the sport more enjoyable and safe for everyone.

4. Be conscious of snow conditions. Some snow conditions are more difficult to ski than others and, as a result, can be more dangerous. Some snow conditions don't lend themselves to experimentation or "go for it" type skiing. When the conditions are icy or wet heavy snow, for example, skiing the bumps should be done cautiously.

5. Take a few easy runs before skiing the bumps. Skiing a few easy runs acts as a warm up. It is imperative to increase the strength and flexibility of your muscles gradually before getting into the more physically demanding aspects of skiing the bumps. A few warm-up runs also lets you get the feel of your skis and hone your technique. You will find a good warm up will make for a more rewarding day of skiing. Note: Some skiers like to stretch before going skiing to increase their flexibility.

6. Know when you are getting tired. Skiing the bumps when you are tired can result in injury. Many times a bump skier will not realize he is getting tired because he is having so much fun. If you find yourself losing concentration or making more skiing errors than usual, you are probably getting tired. This is the time to take a few easy runs on groomed terrain or call it quits for the day.

7. Routinely check your equipment for needed adjustments or any broken parts. This is especially true of bindings. Skiing hard in the bumps can cause equipment to come out of adjustment or sometimes even break. All the top bump skiers check their equipment regularly to make sure it is working properly.

Practicing these few simple points of safety can make the difference between an exciting day of skiing the bumps or a day that ends with injury.

Chapter #12

How To Get In Shape For Skiing The Bumps

Conditioning is the first step to becoming a good bump skier! Being in good shape will not only increase a skier's performance level, but it will also help in the prevention of skiing injuries.

1. Aerobic fitness is a prerequisite. In laymen's terms, aerobic fitness means increasing a person's endurance level by conditioning his cardiovascular system. In other words, increasing the body's ability to pump oxygen rich blood to the muscles so they can perform more efficiently. Bump skiing is really not an aerobic or endurance sport, like cross country skiing, for example. However, aerobic fitness is still a prerequisite. Let me explain why.

Skiing the bumps is primarily an *anerobic* activity. An *anerobic* activity is more of a short spurt or sprinting type of exercise that occurs in between periods of rest. A ski run in the bumps is not unlike a series of sprints. I've timed professional bump skiers skiing the bumps in Sun Valley. The average run is about 30 to 45 seconds long before they stop to take a rest. A 60 second run would be a marathon by comparison. This is hardly an example of an endurance activity. However, it's amazing the amount of energy it takes to ski the bumps for that short a time. A skier who develops his aerobic capacity can recover more rapidly and more often from these *anerobic* type sprints in the bumps. A skier who doesn't develop his aerobic capacity fatigues more rapidly and becomes exhausted after fewer sprints. Aerobic fitness serves well as a base for bump skiing conditioning.

> **Exercises that develop aerobic fitness that are good for bump skiing include:** bicycling, running hills or stairs*, and aerobic dance. An aerobic activity should be done three times a week for at least 20 minutes each session.
>
> *Before running hills or stairs, remember to include stretches in the warm-up that specifically loosen up the Achilles tendons. Running hills or stairs puts an extra strain on these muscles.

2. Weight training to develop muscle strength and skiing power. I don't care what sport a person participates in, weight training is a good way of doing the "homework." Weight training permits isolated conditioning of specific muscles that are emphasized in the athlete's particular sport.

When directing a weight training program to include specialized attention to bump skiing, there are a couple of things the skier should consider. First of all, it is just as important to condition the upper body as it is to condition the lower body. Even though skiing is primarily a "legs" sport, *total* body conditioning is crucial for the prevention of injuries. After all, skiing bumps involves using the entire body. With bump skiing, as with any athletic activity, it is the "weak link in the chain" that often receives the injury.

However, more specifically, bump skiing requires muscle conditioning of shoulders (particularly the deltoids), lower back, stomach, thighs, and hamstrings. When working out with weights, it is important to include excercises that condition these areas.

Another important benefit of weight training is maintaining muscle balance. Oftentimes, when an athlete becomes specialized in a particular sport, certain muscles get used more than others and, as a result, they become more developed. This increased muscle development increases an athlete's strength and power and, therefore, his performance level for his sport. However, opposing muscles that don't get used as much in an athlete's particular sport become disporportionately "weaker" and muscle imbalance can occur. This muscle imbalance can lead to injury. With skiers, the particular concern is maintaining a muscle balance between the thighs and the hamstrings.

In skiing, the hamstrings don't get as much conditioning as the thighs do. As a result, the thighs can become disporportionately stronger than the hamstrings. It should be noted that the thighs are naturally stronger than the hamstrings in most people anyway. However, maintaining muscle balance with well-conditioned hamstrings is important to help prevent knee injuries.

Sample Weight Training Exercises For Bump Skiing Include:

Shoulders - Bench press, military press, push-ups, any excercise that particularly works the front and rear deltoids.
Lower back and stomach - Sit-ups, crunches, incline leg lifts, hanging leg lifts.
Thighs - Squats, leg extensions, leg press.
Hamstrings - Leg curls, heel lifts.

Note: Weight training should be done two or three times a week. If a person is active in another sporting activity, such as skiing, weight training twice a week will sufficiently compliment the sport. However, to get ready for the ski season, weight training three times a week is suggested. Weight training for skiing in the pre-season more than three times a week I find is a "burn-out."

One last word on weight training. If a person is experiencing any pain from a particular exercise other than muscle soreness (which is typical from weight training), he should discontinue the exercise. An exercise, even if done properly, can sometimes cause pain because of the particularities of a person's individual body structure. If pain is experienced in an exercise, especially if the pain is in a joint, that exercise should be supplemented with another exercise that works the same muscles, but does not cause pain. With a little experimentation in the gym, a skier can find the right exercises for his particular physique.

3. Stretching to maintain flexibility and reduce injuries. To increase or maintain good flexibility for skiing bumps, stretching should be incorporated into a skier's conditioning routine. Good muscle flexibility aids in the prevention of muscle strains. When stretching, it is important not to bounce or force a stretch. But rather, a stretch should be done gradually. It is a recommended practice to stretch before doing any athletic activity. However, stretching after exercising is important also. Stretching after a vigorous work out makes for a good warm down.

A skier should try to maintain total body flexibility. But specific areas of concern for bump skiing include shoulders, thighs, groin, hamstrings, back, and hips. Incorporate stretches that target these areas.

Let me make one final point about conditioning. It is common for a skier to become over enthusiastic about his sport. However, he should be careful not to overtax himself with physical activity in an attempt to increase his overall skiing conditioning. Days of rest should be incorporated into any conditioning routine to let the muscles rebuild themselves. These days of rest are imperative to athletic improvement!

Chapter #13

Ten Common Errors Made When Skiing The Bumps

1. Not being in shape. The first problem some skiers have to skiing the bumps well is that they are simply out of shape. They tire quickly in the bumps and, as a result, their skiing skill level rapidly declines. (See Chapter 12, "How To Get In Shape For Skiing The Bumps.")

2. Jumping in over one's head. Some skiers have an impatient perception of their skiing ability. The best way to learn how to ski bumps is by working on a progression. So, start in small bumps first. Practice skiing in smaller, more manageable bumps before applying these techniques to more radical terrain.

3. Not breathing. A mistake some skiers make while skiing the bumps is they will literally hold their breath. This involuntary reflex is somewhere along the lines of closing one's eyes when doing a somersault. If a skier holds his breath while skiing bumps, this significantly reduces the amount of oxygen going to the muscles. This reduces the muscles performance level. And, therefore, the skier's performance, or at least his endurance level when skiing bumps. When skiing bumps, concentrate on breathing rhythmically. More specifically, remember to "blow out." Breathing in will come more automatically.

4. Weak edge setting turns. When skiing in the bumps, an indication of weak edge setting turns is the skier having difficulty controlling speed and maintaining fall line skiing. This is especially evident when there is a transition to steeper terrain. Remember, when skiing over a transition to steeper terrain in the bumps, a skier will have to compensate by making harder edge sets in his turns to maintain a controlled speed. Otherwise, his skiing speed can build to an uncontrolled point very rapidly. The effect is like a snowball rolling downhill. The steeper the incline, the faster the snowball rolls. Skiing bumps requires strong edge setting type turns. (See Chapter 6, "How To Make Controlled Turns In The Bumps")

5. Favoring one leg. It is common for even an experienced skier to favor his stronger, more coordinated leg. In the bumps, this can result with the skier having weak turns to one side. To maintain a controlled speed in the bumps requires strong edge setting type turns in *both* directions. Oftentimes, correction is just developing an awareness of the imbalance. Concentration on making harder edge sets on the skier's weaker turning side will often correct the problem.

6. Not keeping the weight on the downhill ski. Some skiers put such a high priority on keeping their feet together that they inadvertently become even-weighted on their skis. As a result, they put too much weight on the uphill ski. Having weight on the uphill ski can cause a couple of problems when skiing the bumps. First, skiers who put too much weight on the uphill ski have a tendency to cross tails in the bumps. Also, these skiers tend to lean into the hill which can cause the skis to "jet" or slip out from underneath them when making turns in the bumps. Concentrate on keeping the weight on the downhill ski when skiing bumps.

7. Not driving forward with the hands. Being able to keep the hands in front of the body is important to skiing bumps well. If a skier lets his hands get back or even to the side of his body, then he is back on his skis and, therefore, off balance. Skiers who have had any experience skiing bumps are aware of this principle. However, many times unexpectedly their hands can still get knocked back. Put energy into driving forward with the hands. (See Chapter 8, "The Importance Of The Pole Plant.")

8. Blocking the turns. Sometimes a skier will block his turns by trying to turn too fast. Blocking the turns occurs when a skier tries to make another turn before he has finished the preceeding one. The result can often be no turn at all. Skiing bumps requires fast feet that can initiate alot of turns. However, some skiers try to get this fast foot action by resorting to a foot swiveling technique. Foot swivel is more cosmetic than functional because the ski does not carve the turn. But rather, it slides or pivots the turn. Ironically, a common consequence of foot swiveling is blocked turns. The upper body is doing alot of wiggling, but there isn't much deflection in the skis. This makes it difficult to control speed in the bumps. If a skier finds himself blocking his turns, simply calm down and concentrate on making good edge setting type turns. Sometimes this will mean waiting just a little bit in between some turns to turn on the most convenient part of the bump. Surprisingly, the skier will be amazed how fast his turns will be when he lets his skis help do some of the work.

9. Improperly canted boots. To achieve the most control in one's skiing, the skier has to be able to make strong edge sets in his turns. Getting good edge sets in the turns can be impaired if the skier is skiing in improperly canted boots. An indication of a skier who is skiing in improperly canted boots is a skier who habitually skis either with knock-knees or bow legs. Many people, if not most people, were not born with perfectly straight legs. As a result, most skiers require the aid of boot canting to compensate for individual leg structure. Different ski boots come with different pre-determined cants. It is important that this pre-determined cant is the correct cant for the individual skier. A boot's canting should always be considered before purchase. However, if a skier wants to know if his present boots are properly canted to his individual specifications, that can be simply determined at most ski shops. Note: Some ski shop personnel may want to cant the skier by canting his bindings. This does achieve the desired canting, however, this procedure can affect the binding mounting and release characteristics. With the many models of ski boots available, some of which have adjustments for canting built into the boot. This writer feels canting the boot is the most effective canting procedure.

10. "Ah yes, the 'pound'." Some skiers have the tendency to "pound" their way down the bumps. The cause for this is not extending enough on the back sides of the bumps. As a result, these skiers drop down or "pound" from one bump to the next. To get proper extension in the bumps, especially larger ones, push the tips of the skis down to the snow and get good hip projection. (See Chapter 7, "How To Absorb And Extend In Big Bumps.")

Conclusion
Self Evaluation

In this last chapter, I would like to make a point about the psychology of sport, and how it applies to attaining a desired proficiency in bump skiing. Once a skier attains a certain skiing proficiency, improvement or at least maintenance of that skiing level, becomes an exercise in objective error detection. The key word here is *objective*. Let me explain.

When skiing bumps, the skier needs to view his skiing ability with an objective eye. This is especially important when the skier makes an error. When the skier makes an error in his skiing, he can not let his mind become cluttered with non-specific self-criticisms. Criticisms like, "I'm just a lousy skier" or "I always fall down in the bumps." Self-criticisms like these are more concerned with personal value judgments than with skiing improvement. These types of self-criticisms mentally hinder an objective error detection process when a skiing error is made.

When a skiing error is made the skier should not worry about its social impact, but rather he should seek the *technical cause* of the error. The technical cause of a skiing error or fall would be too much weight on the uphill ski, for example. Seeking the technical cause of a skiing error will lead to skiing improvement because once a skier detects the cause of a sking error he can then CORRECT IT! In the example I just gave, once the skier realizes he has put too much weight on the uphill ski, he then can correct the skiing error by putting more weight on the downhill ski.

When working with an objective error correction process, it is best to work on correcting one thing at a time. Example: Stronger edge sets at the end of the turns. Trying to correct more than one thing at a time makes concentration difficult. Fortunately, working on one skiing problem at a time will often aid in the correction, if not correct, other bad habits as well.

Finally, one other point about correcting bump skiing errors. Don't be afraid to intersperse a few runs on groomed terrain to work out kinks in technique. Even professional bump skiers rely on the benefits of groomed terrain to help hone their bump skiing skills.

In closing, let me say to become a good bump skier takes *practice!* But what fun practice! Hopefully, the information in this book will enable the reader to attain the same enjoyment in skiing bumps that I have been able to enjoy over the last ten years. So have fun, and have a good day skiing!